T0084231

THE BEST OF
RICHARD CLAYDERMAN

HAL•LEONARD®
CORPORATION
7777 W. BLUEMOUND RD. P.O. BOX 13819 MILWAUKEE, WI 53213

BALLADE POUR ADELINE

Music by
PAUL DE SENNEVILLE

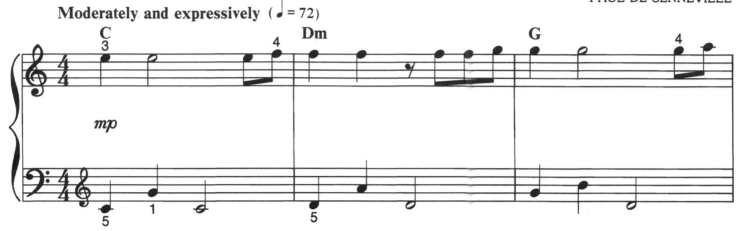

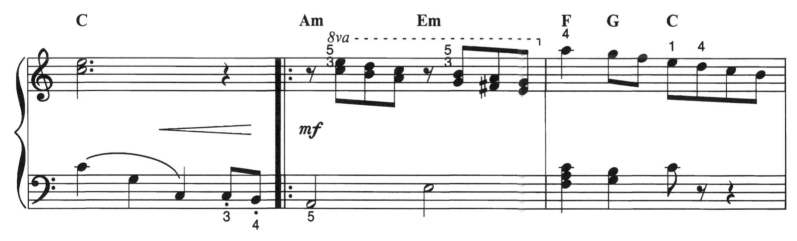

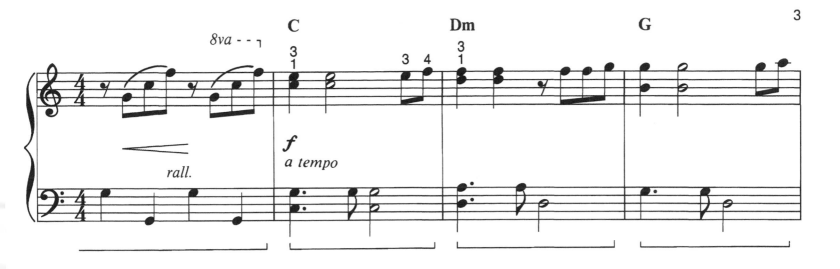

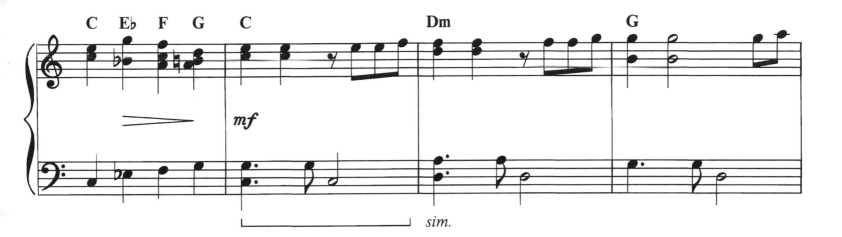

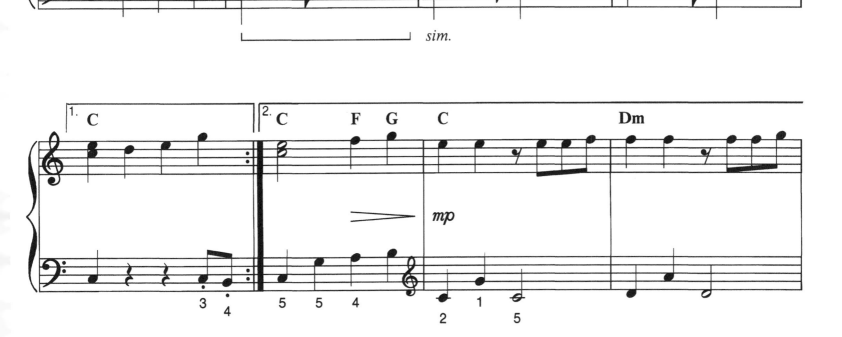

DON'T CRY FOR ME ARGENTINA

(From the opera "EVITA")

Lyric by TIM RICE
Music by ANDREW LLOYD WEBBER

Moderate Tango tempo

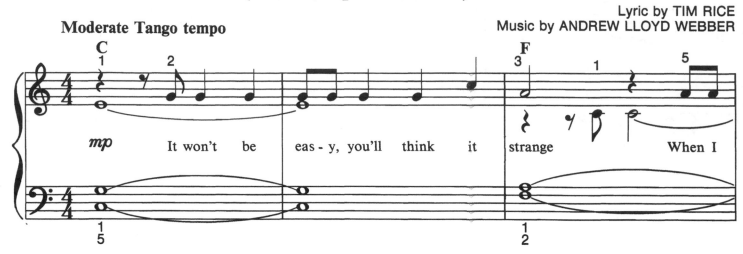

mp It won't be eas-y, you'll think it strange When I

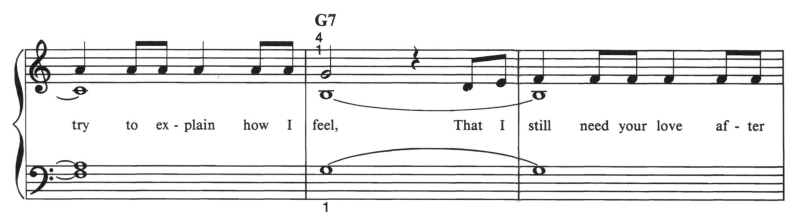

try to ex-plain how I feel, That I still need your love af-ter

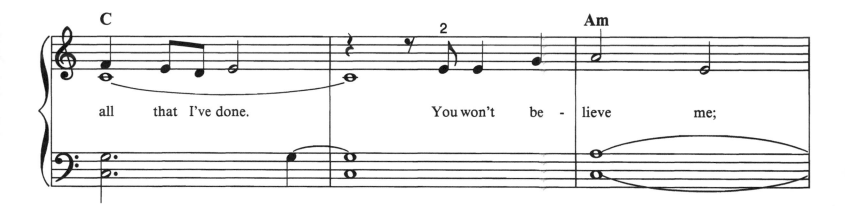

all that I've done. You won't be-lieve me;

All you will see is a girl you once knew al-though she's dressed up to the

nines   at   six - es   and   sev - ens   with   you.

I had to let it   hap - pen, I had   to   change;   Could - n't
And as   for   for - tune and as for   fame,   I

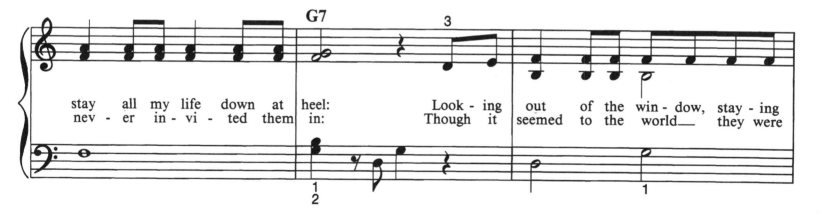

stay   all my life down at   heel: Look - ing   out of the win - dow, stay - ing
nev - er in - vi - ted them in: Though it seemed to the world___ they were

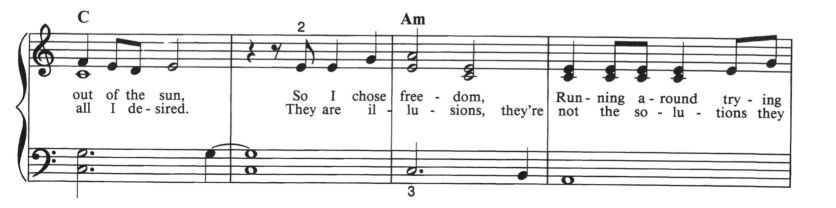

out   of the sun,   So I chose free - dom,   Run - ning a - round   try - ing
all   I de - sired.   They are il - lu - sions, they're   not the so - lu - tions they

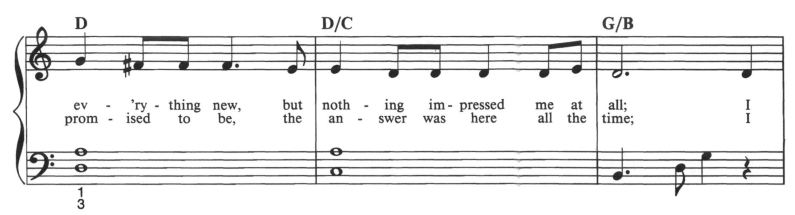

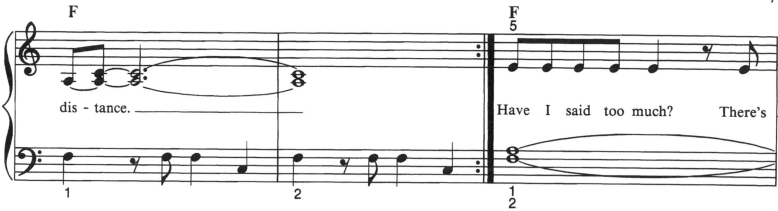

dis - tance. _____ Have I said too much? There's

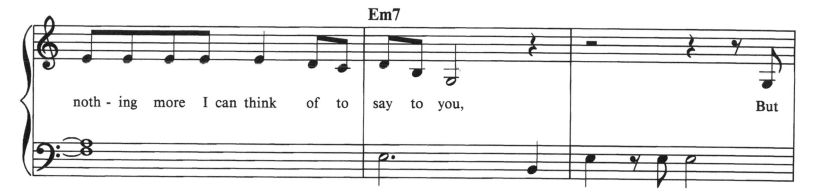

noth - ing more I can think of to say to you, But

all you have to do is look at me to know that ev - 'ry word is true.

CODA

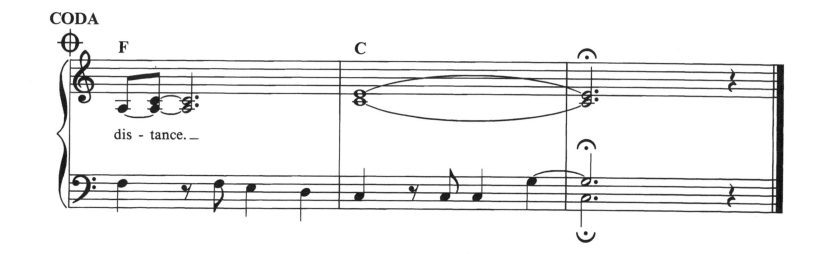

dis - tance. _

HARMONY

Music by
PAUL DE SENNEVILLE

Moderately and expressively (♩ = 69)

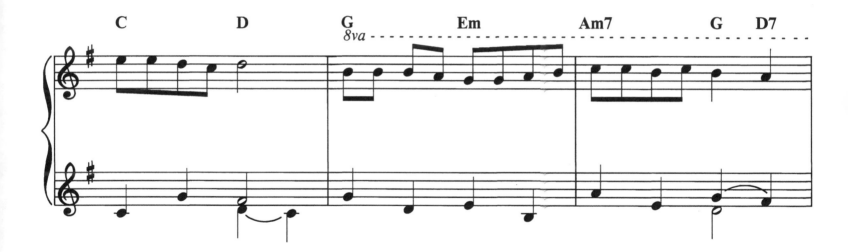

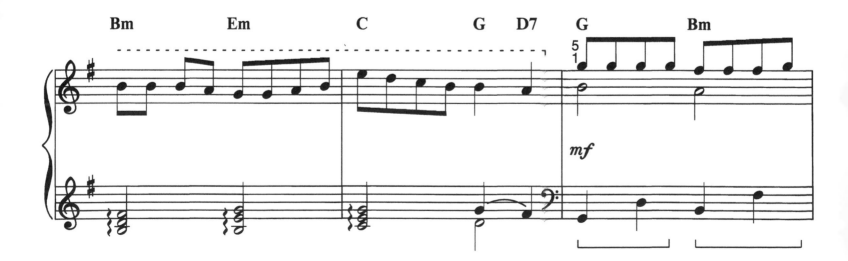

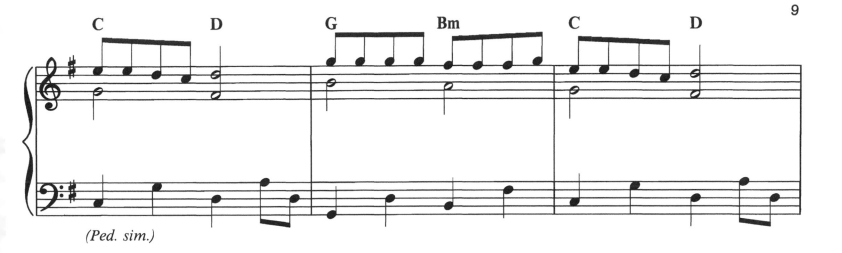

(Ped. sim.)

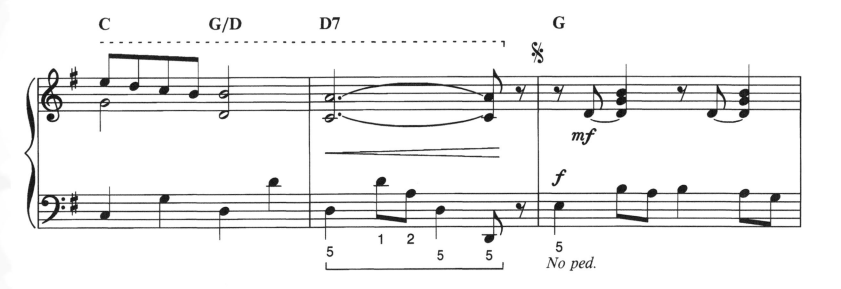

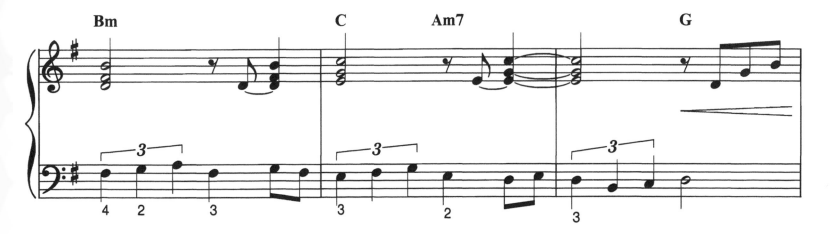

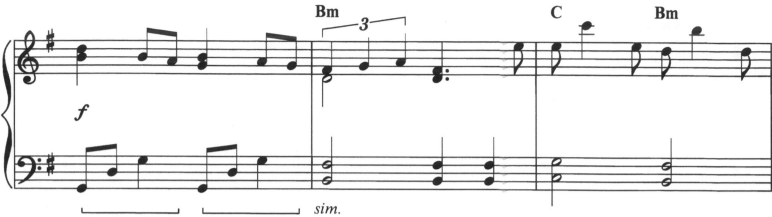

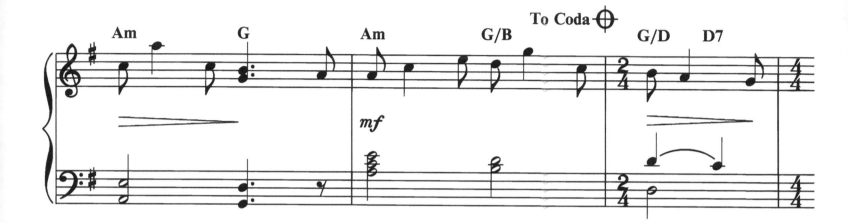

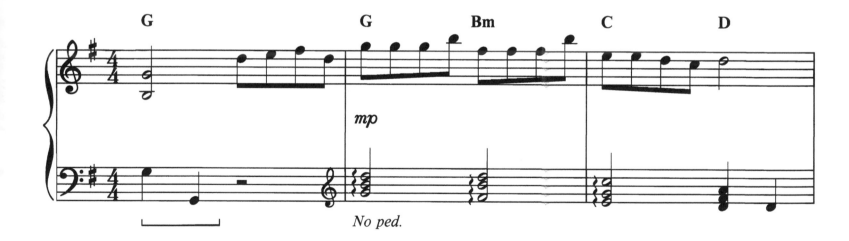

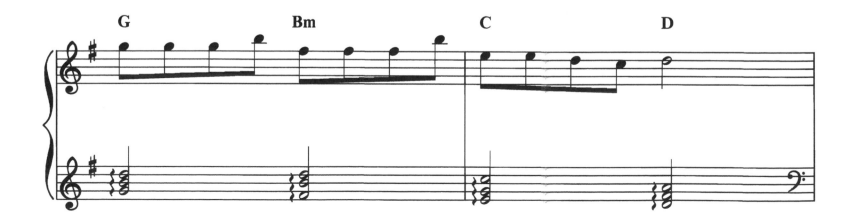

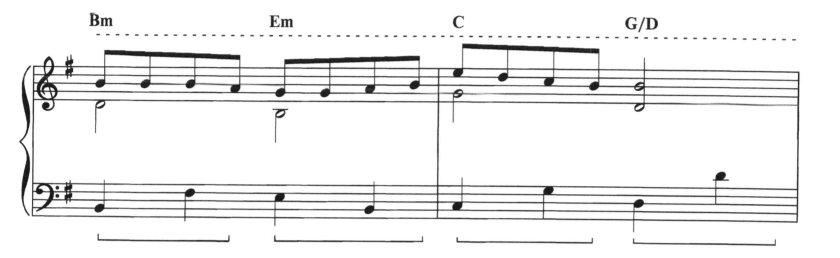

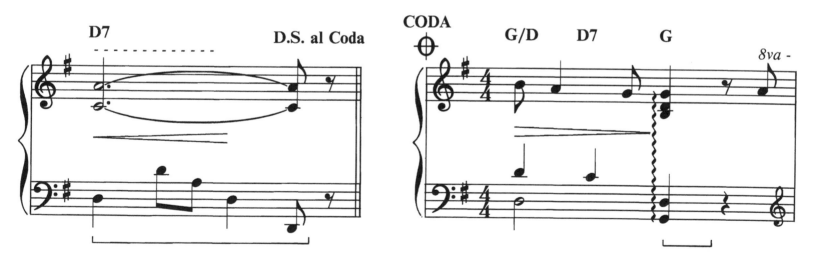

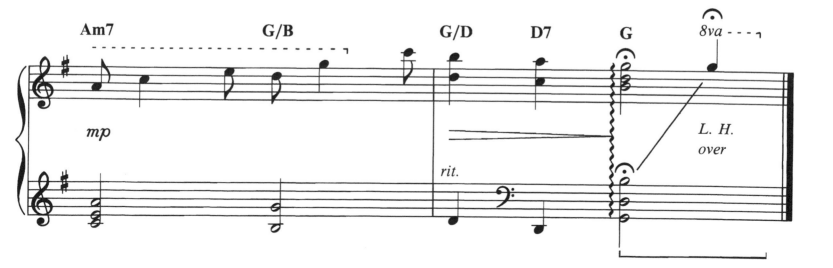

HELLO

Words and Music by
LIONEL RICHIE

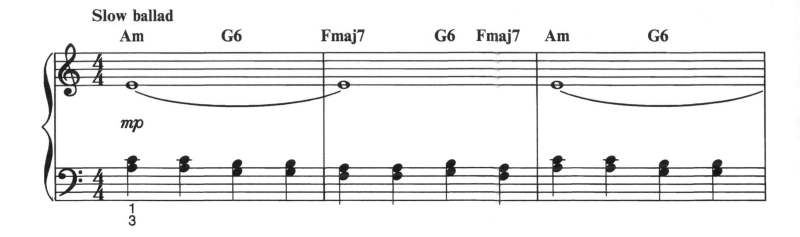

I've been a-lone with you in-side my mind And
long to see the sun-light in your hair And

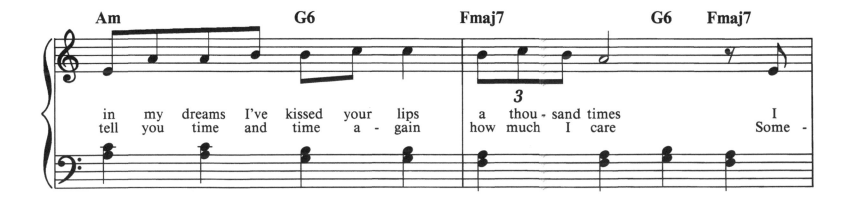

in my dreams I've kissed your lips a thou-sand times I
tell you time and time a-gain how much I care Some-

13

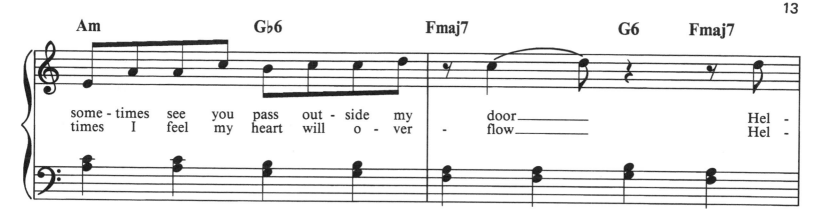

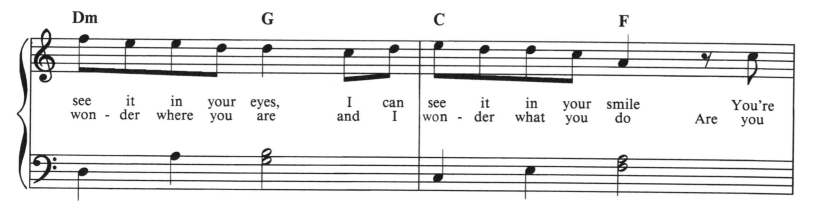

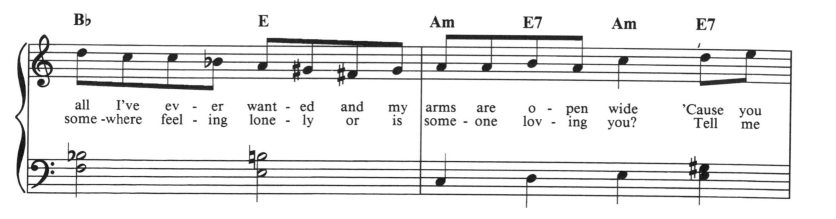

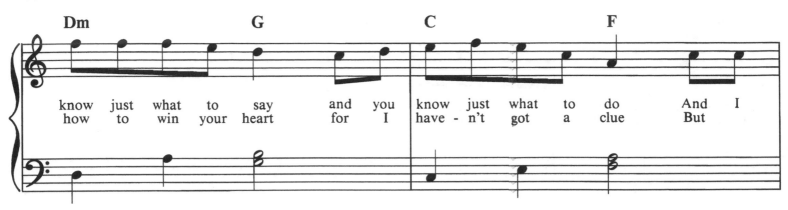

know just what to say and you know just what to do And I
how to win your heart for I have-n't got a clue But

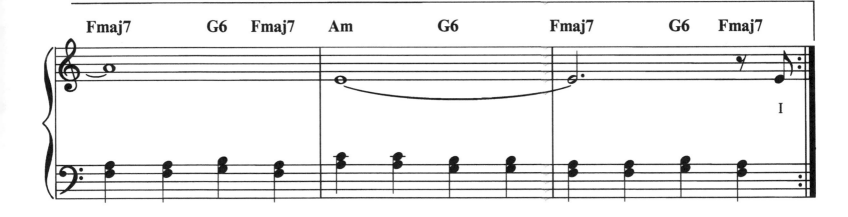

want to tell you so much, I love you.
let me start by say-ing, I love

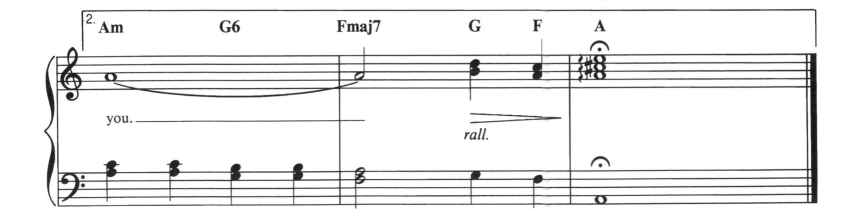

you.

rall.

HOW DEEP IS YOUR LOVE

Words and Music by BARRY GIBB,
ROBIN GIBB and MAURICE GIBB

Moderate soft rock beat

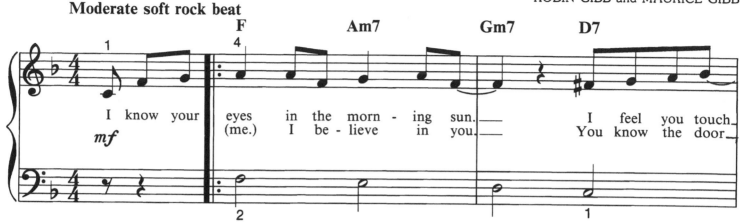

I know your eyes in the morn-ing sun.___ I feel you touch___
(me.) I be-lieve in you.___ You know the door___

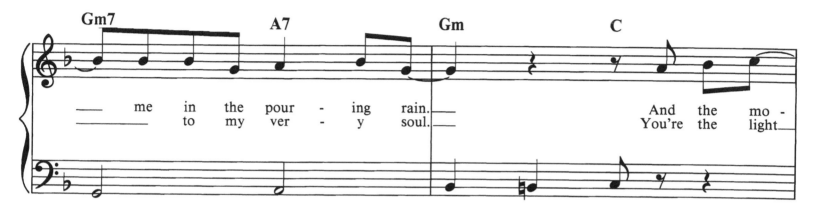

___ me in the pour-ing rain.___ And the mo - light___
___ to my ver - y soul.___ You're the light___

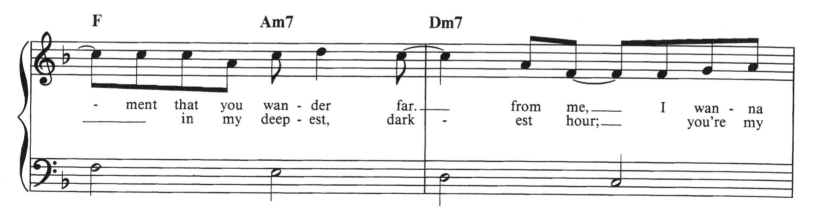

- ment that you wan-der far.___ from me,___ I wan-na
___ in my deep-est, dark - est hour;___ you're my

feel you in my arms a - gain.___ And you
sav - ior___ when I fall.___ And you

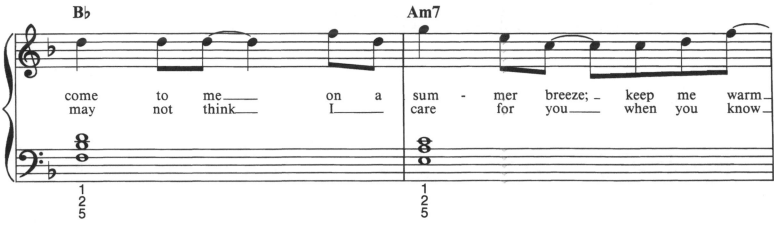

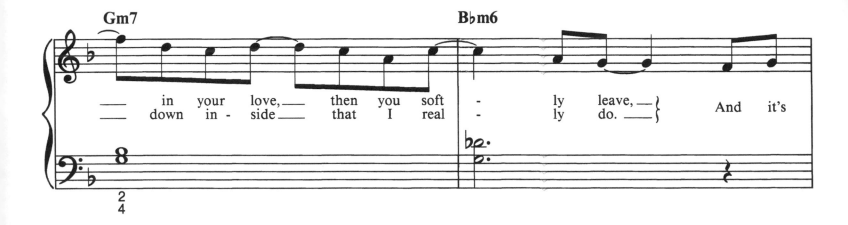

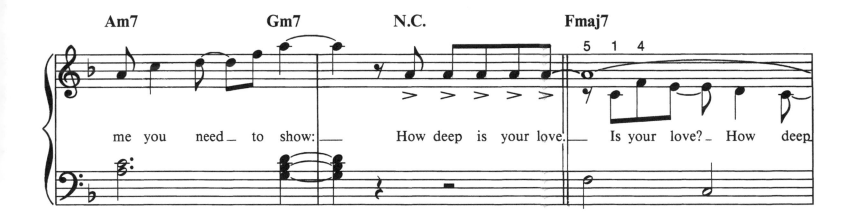

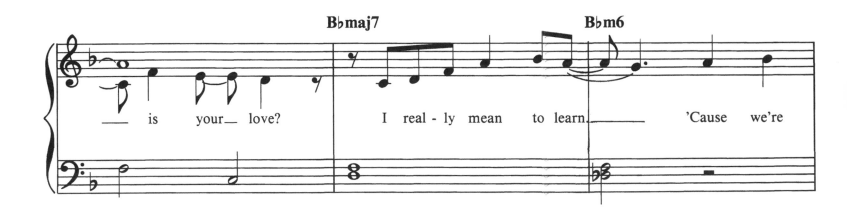

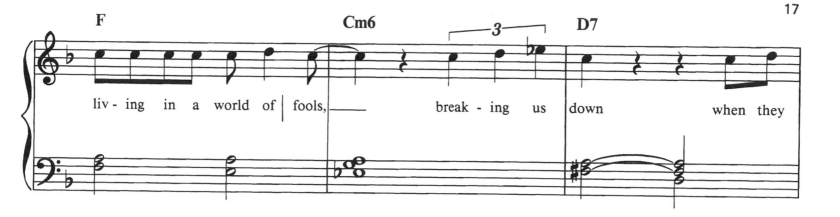

living in a world of fools, _____ break-ing us down when they

all should let us be. _____ We be-long _____ to you and

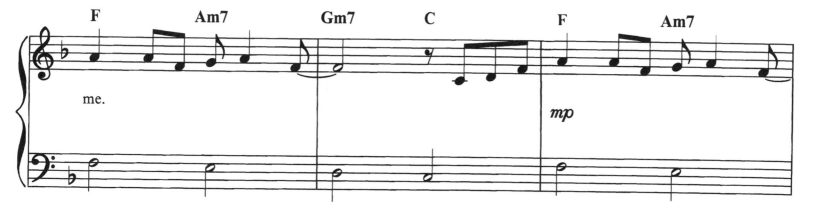

me.

I HAVE A DREAM

Words and Music by BENNY ANDERSSON
and BJÖRN ULVAEUS

Moderate, flowing style

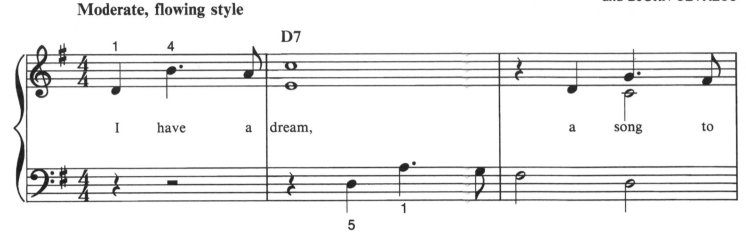

I have a dream, a song to

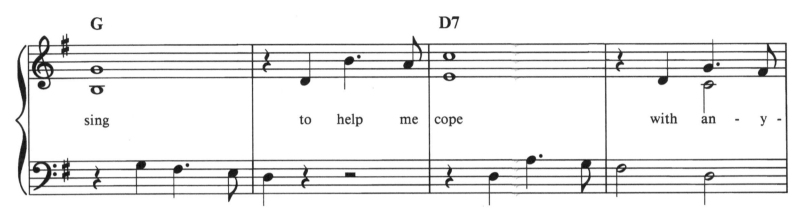

sing to help me cope with an-y-

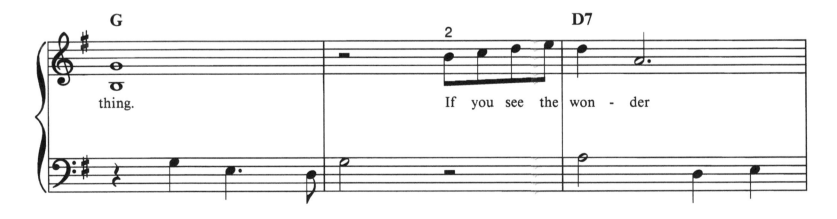

thing. If you see the won - der

of a fair - y tale, you can take the

fu - ture   e - ven if you fail.

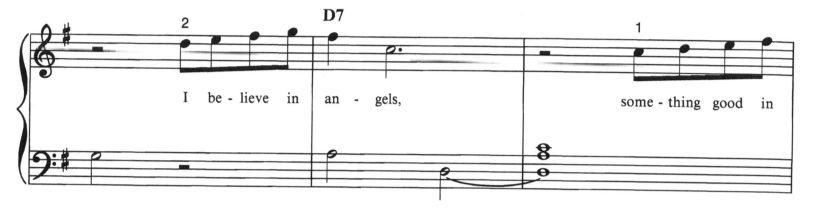

I be - lieve in an - gels,   some - thing good in

ev - 'ry - thing I see.   I be - lieve in an - gels

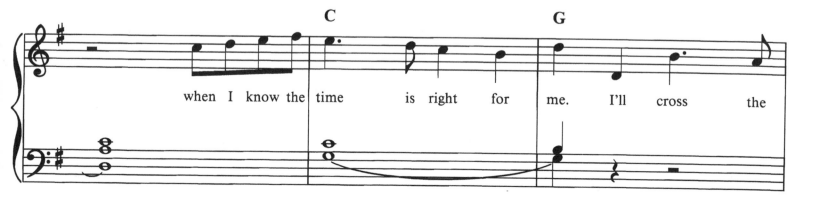

when I know the time   is right for   me. I'll   cross   the

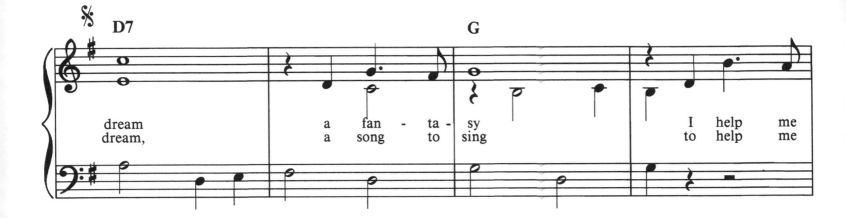

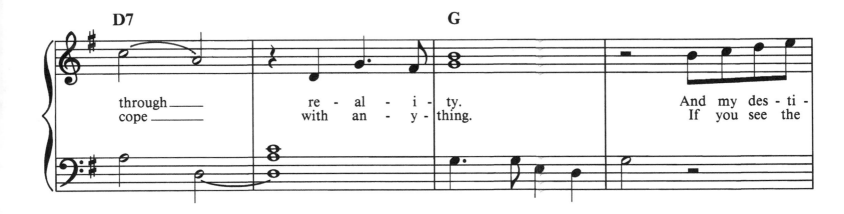

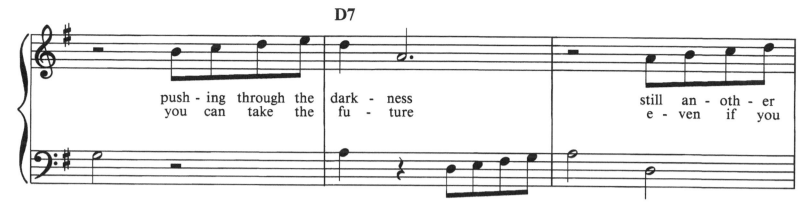

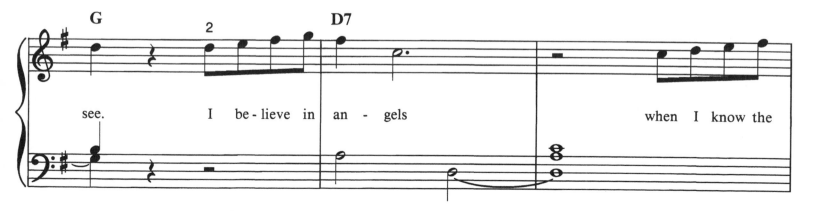

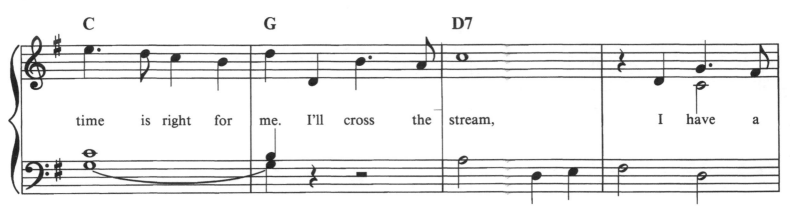

time   is   right   for   me.   I'll   cross   the   stream,   I   have   a

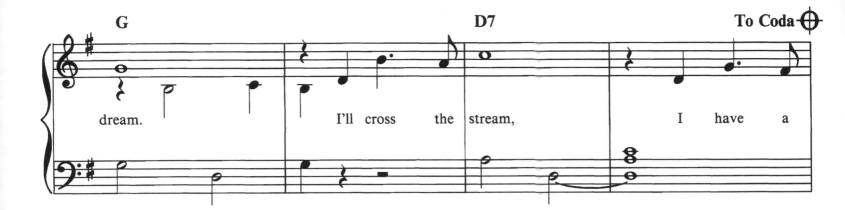

dream.   I'll   cross   the   stream,   I   have   a

dream.   I   have   a

dream.   *rit.*

LA VIE EN ROSE

Original French Words by EDITH PIAF
English Words by MACK DAVID
Music by LOUIGUY

Freely

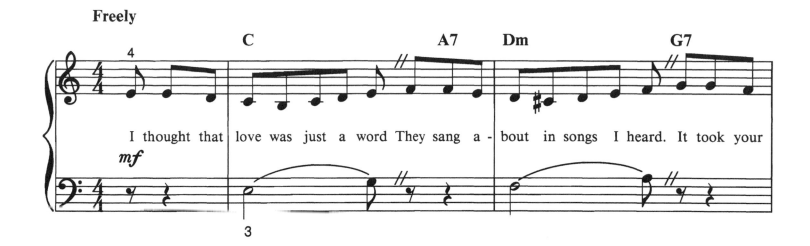

I thought that love was just a word They sang a - bout in songs I heard. It took your *mf* kiss -

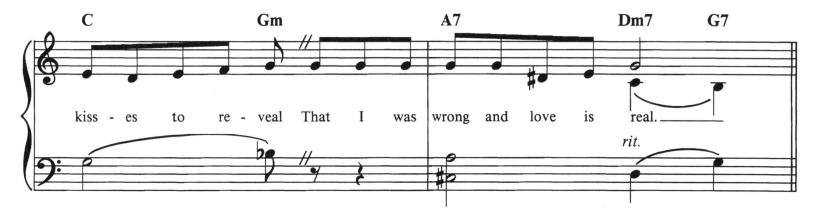

kiss - es to re - veal That I was wrong and love is real. *rit.*

Chorus
Slowly, with expression

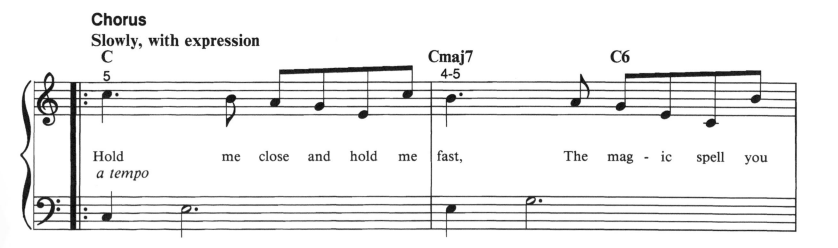

Hold me close and hold me fast, The mag - ic spell you
a tempo

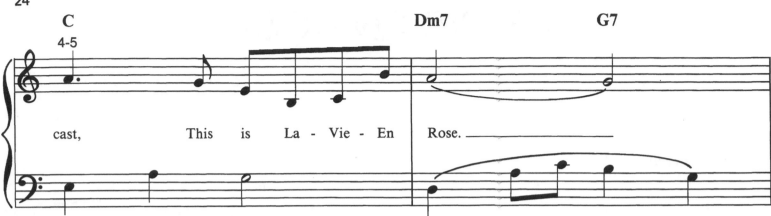

cast, This is La - Vie - En Rose. _____

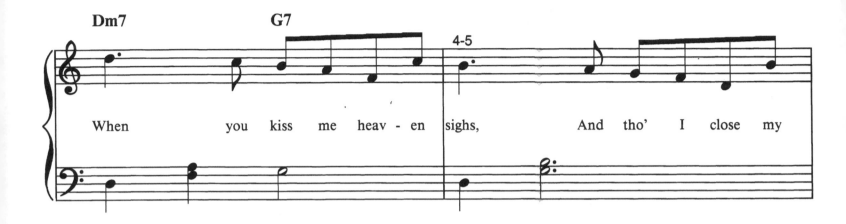

When you kiss me heav - en sighs, And tho' I close my

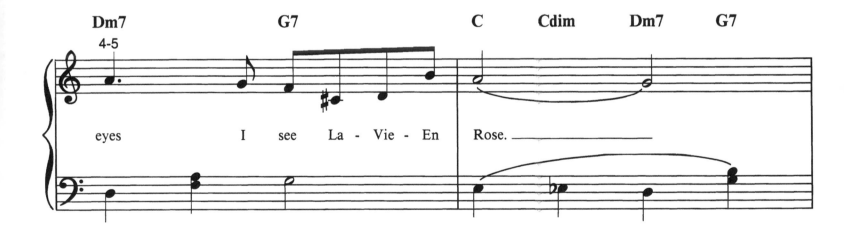

eyes I see La - Vie - En Rose. _____

When you press me to your heart I'm in a world a -

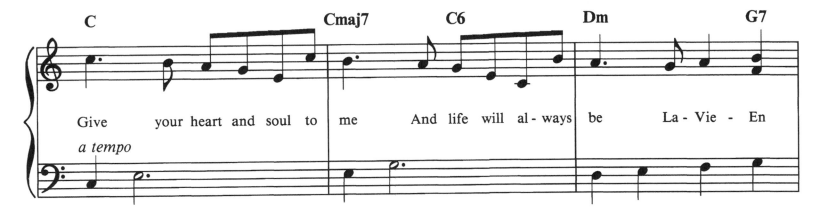

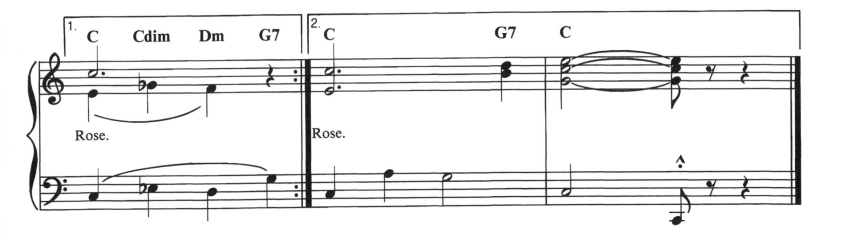

LARA'S THEME

Words by PAUL FRANCIS WEBSTER
Music by MAURICE JARRE

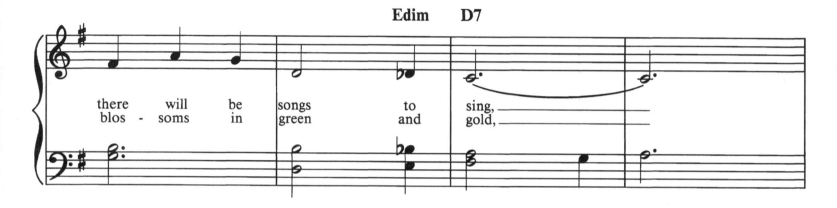

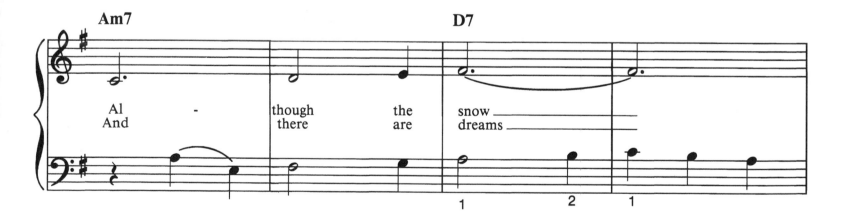

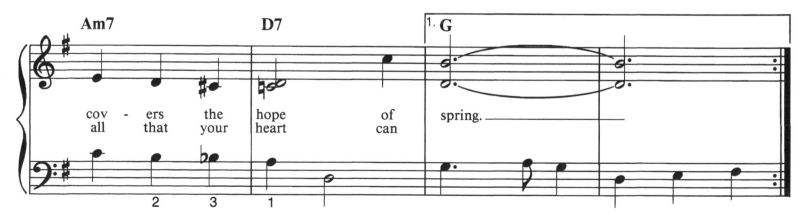

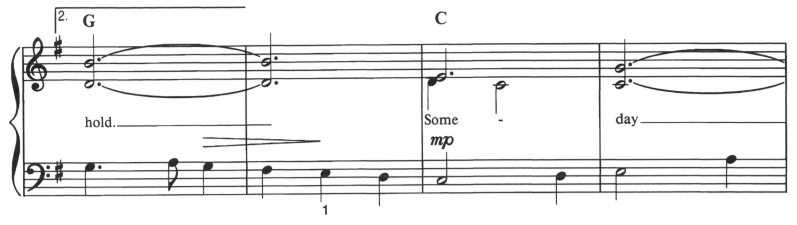

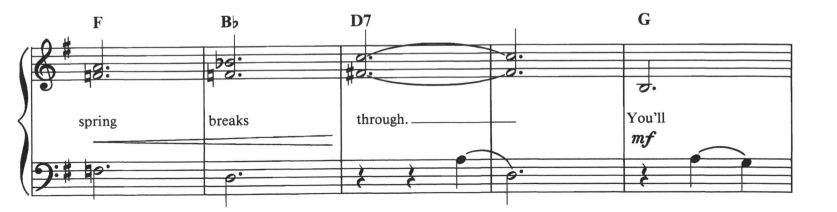

Edim

come to me___ out of the long a -

D7   Am   D7

go,___ Warm as the wind,___

G

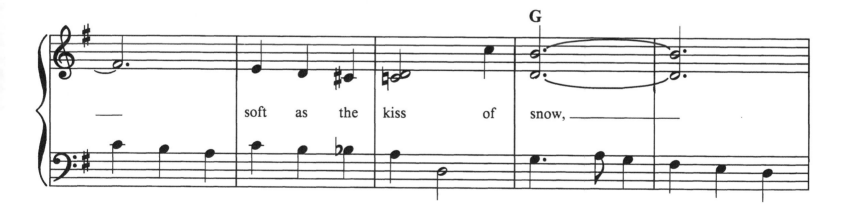

___ soft as the kiss of snow,___

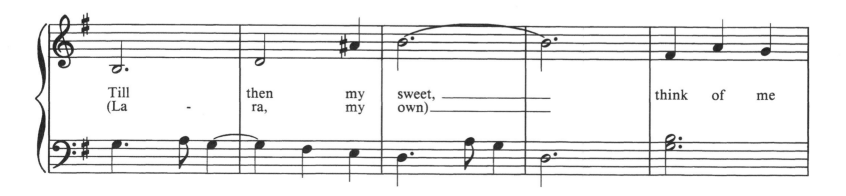

Till then my sweet,___ think of me
(La - ra, my own)___

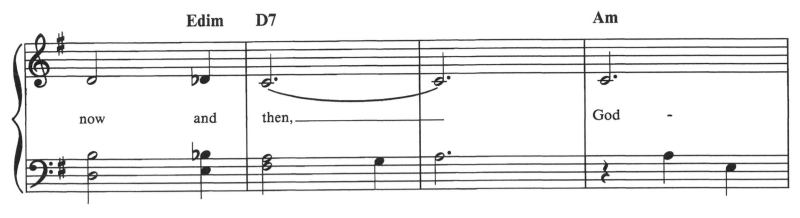

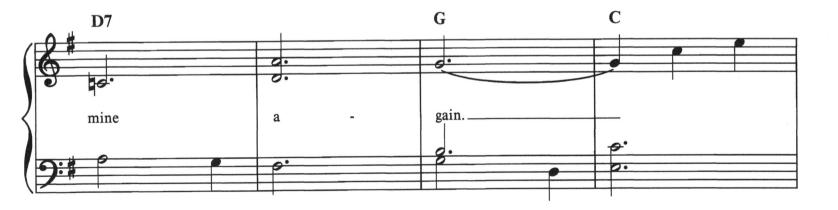

LOVE IS BLUE
(L'amour Est Bleu)

English Lyric by BRIAN BLACKBURN
Original French Lyric by PIERRE COUR
Music by ANDRE POPP

Moderately slow, easy feel

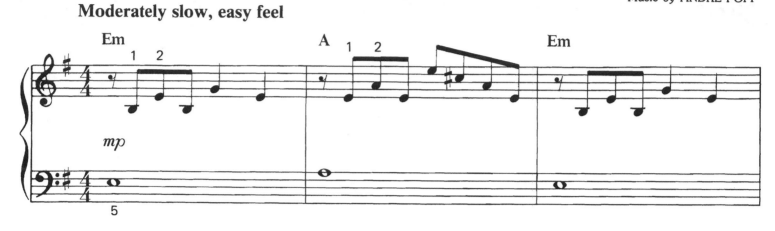

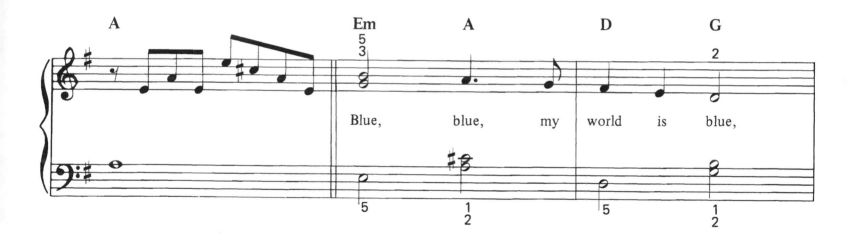

life is grey, Cold is my heart since you went a - way.

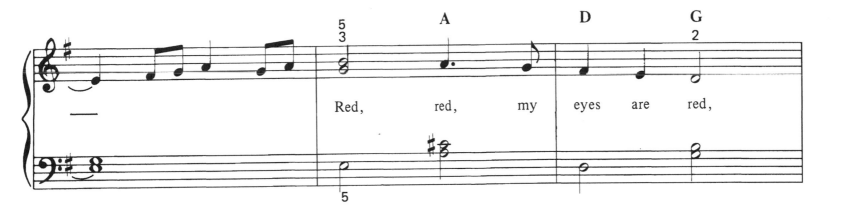

Red, red, my eyes are red,

Cry - ing for you a - lone in my bed. Green, green, my

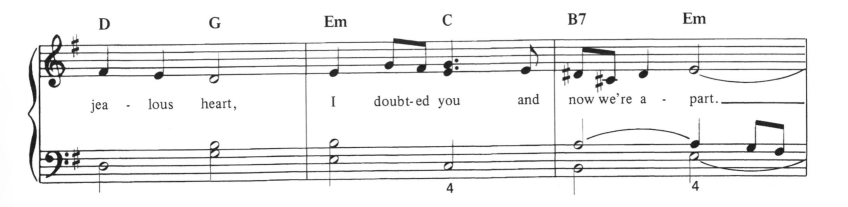

jea - lous heart, I doubt-ed you and now we're a - part.

More broadly

When we met, how the

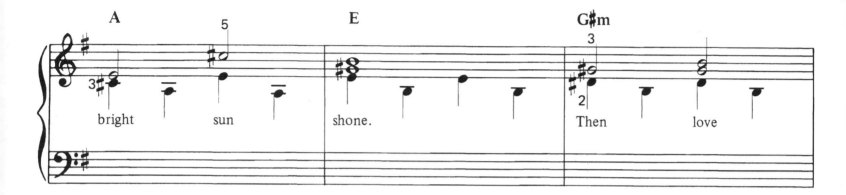

bright sun shone. Then love

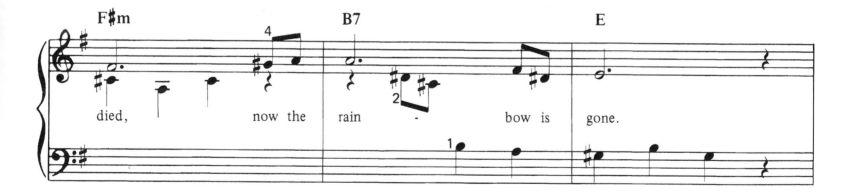

died, now the rain - bow is gone.

As before

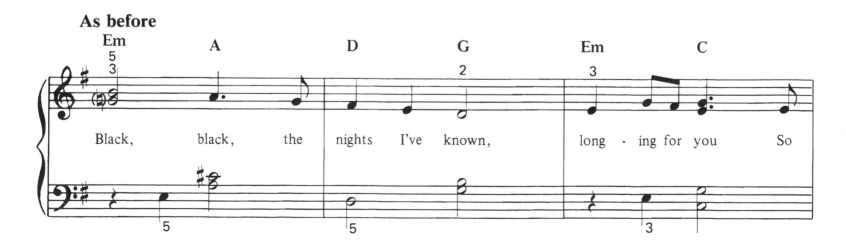

Black, black, the nights I've known, long - ing for you So

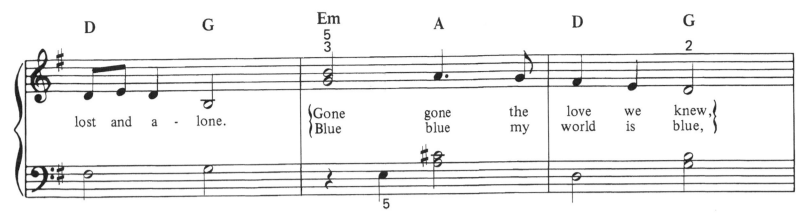

lost and a - lone. {Gone gone the love we knew,}
{Blue blue my world is blue,}

Blue is my world now I'm with-out you.____

I'm with-out you.____
rall.- - - - - - - - - - - - - -

Repeat and Fade

a tempo

LOVE STORY

Words by CARL SIGMAN
Music by FRANCIS LAI

Moderately, expressively

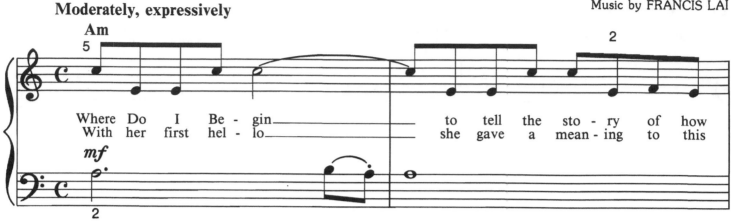

Where Do I Be - gin _____ to tell the sto - ry of how
With her first hel - lo _____ she gave a mean - ing to this

great a love can be, _____ The sweet love sto - ry that is old - er than the sea,
emp - ty world of mine; _____ There'd nev - er be an - oth - er love, an - oth - er time;

The sim - ple truth a - bout the love she brings to me? _____ Where do I
She came in - to my life and made the liv - ing fine. _____

start? _____

She fills my heart, _____

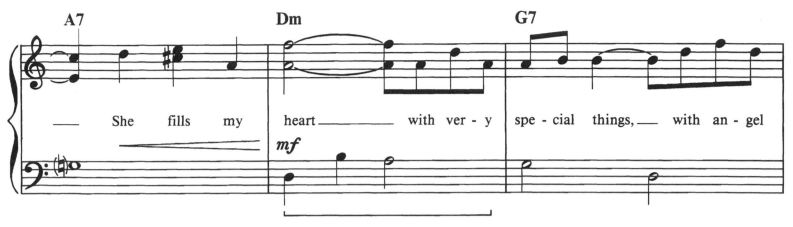

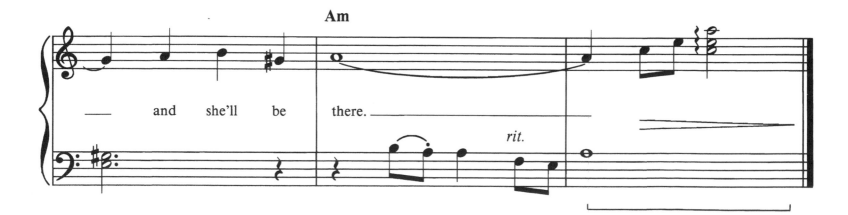

MEMORY

(From "CATS")

Text by TREVOR NUNN after T.S. ELIOT
Music by ANDREW LLOYD WEBBER

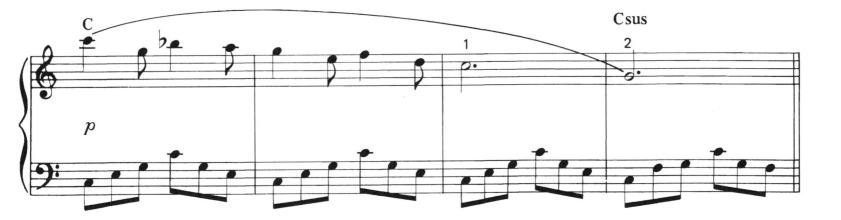

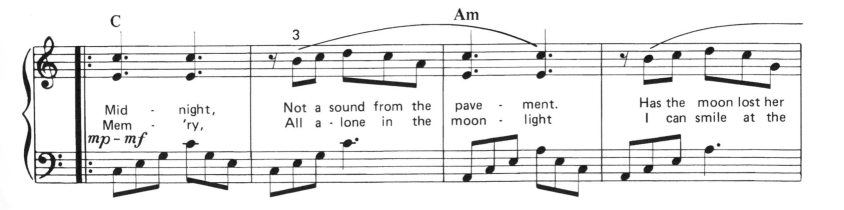

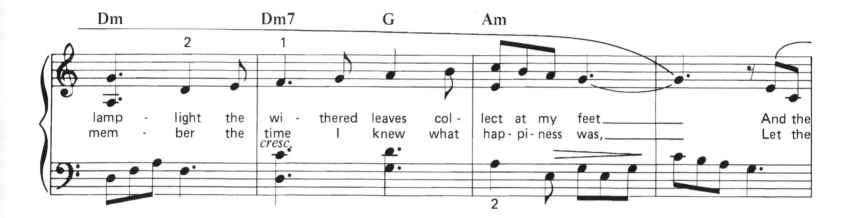

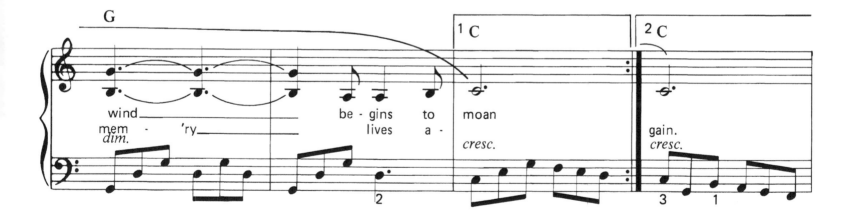

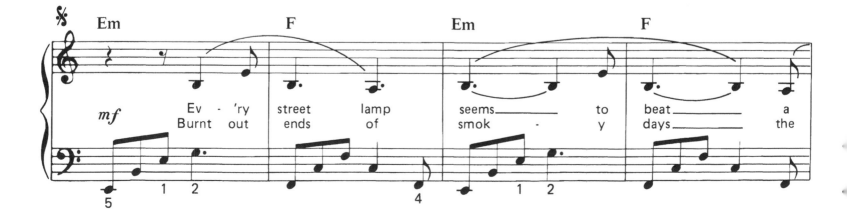

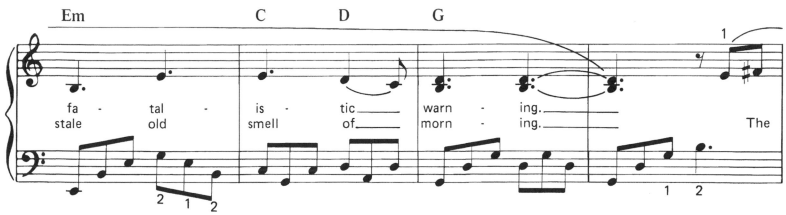

fa - tal - is - tic____ warn - ing.____
stale old smell of____ morn - ing.____ The

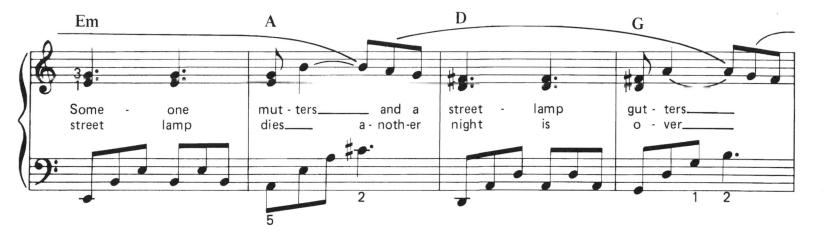

Some - one mut - ters____ and a street - lamp gut - ters____
street lamp dies____ a - noth-er night is o - ver____

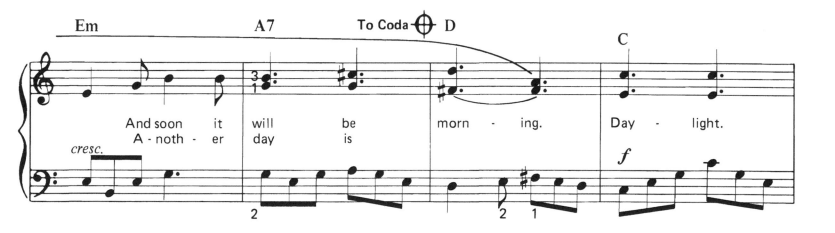

And soon it will be morn - ing. Day - light.
A - noth - er day is

I must wait for the sun - rise I must think of a new life

And I must-n't give in. When the dawn comes to-

night will be a mem-o-ry too And a new day

dim.

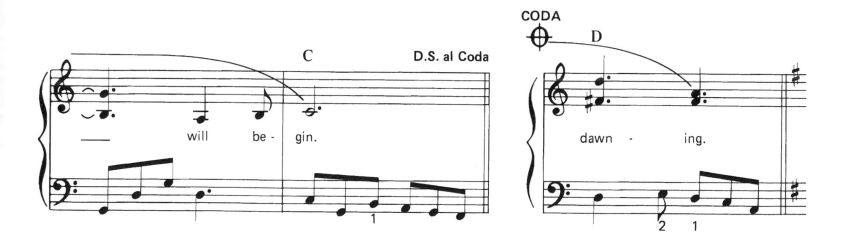

will be-gin.

D.S. al Coda

CODA

dawn - ing.

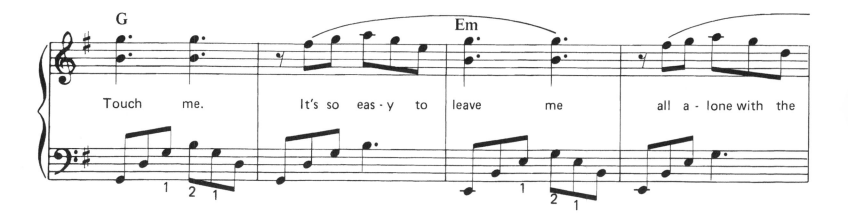

Touch me. It's so eas-y to leave me all a-lone with the

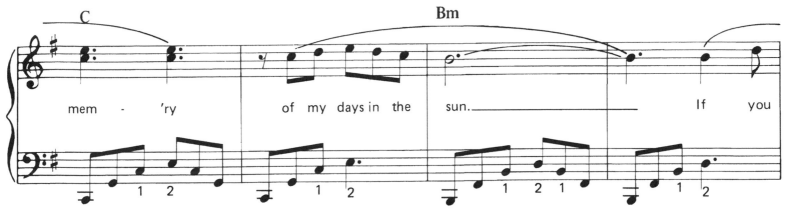

mem - 'ry of my days in the sun._____ If you

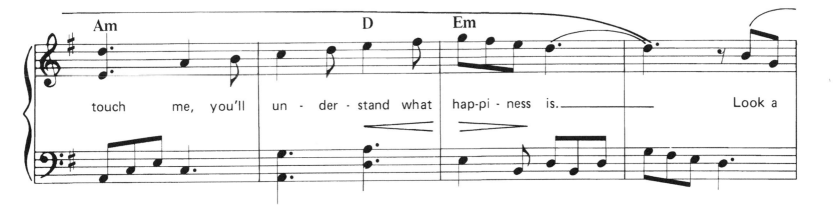

touch me, you'll un - der - stand what hap-pi - ness is._____ Look a

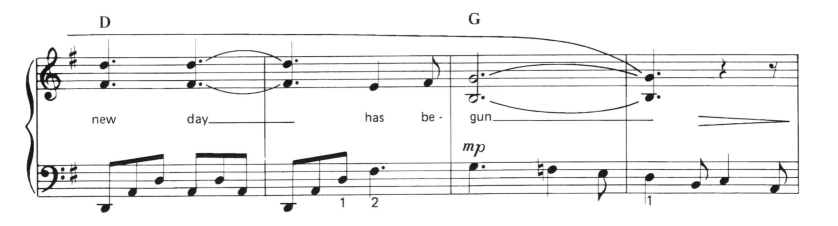

new day_____ has be - gun_____

MOON RIVER

Words by JOHNNY MERCER
Music by HENRY MANCINI

Moderately, in a smooth 3

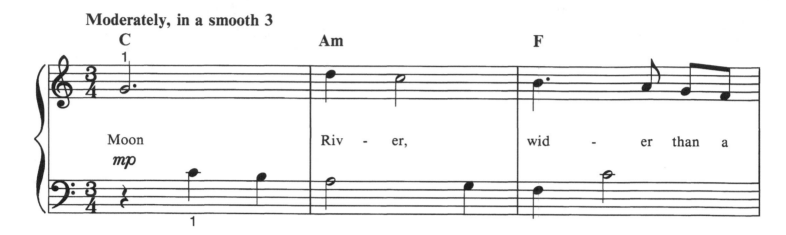

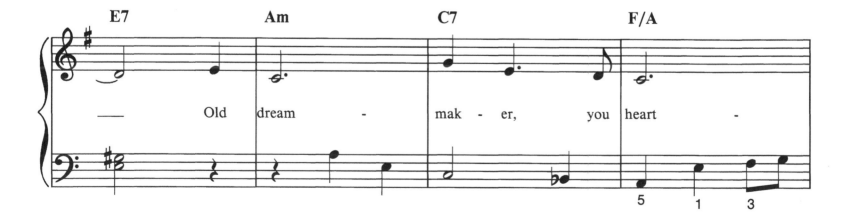

Fm — break-er, — Am/E — wher-ev-er you're — Am6 B7 — go-in', I'm — Em7 A7 — go-in' your

Dm7 G7 — way: — C — Two — Am — drift-ers, — F — off to see the

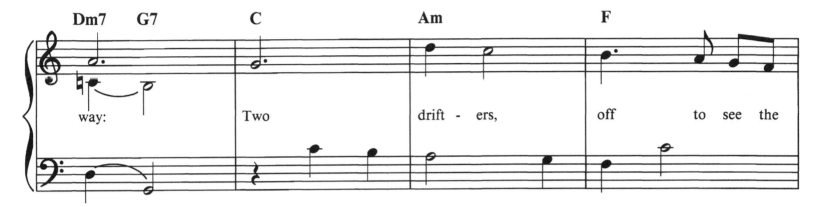

C — world. There's — F — such a lot of — C — world to

Dm6 — see. — E7 — We're — Am — aft - — Am7 — er the

43

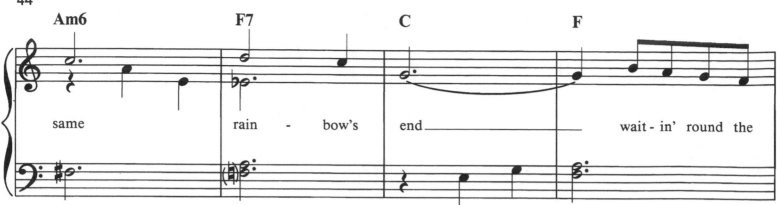

same rain - bow's end _____ wait - in' round the

bend _____ my Huck - le - ber - ry friend, Moon

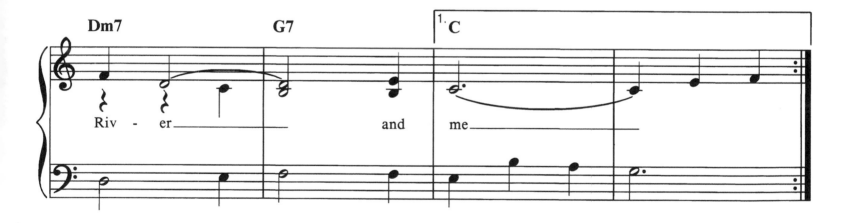

Riv - er _____ and me _____

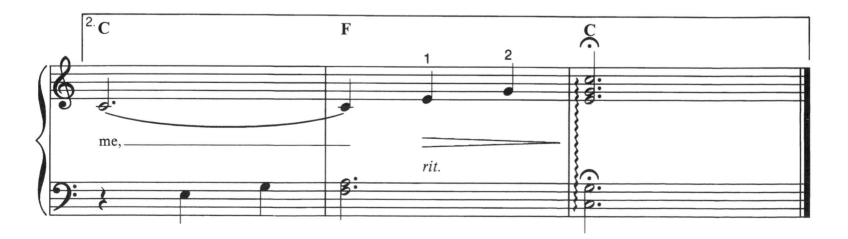

me, _____ rit.

STRANGERS IN THE NIGHT

Words by CHARLES SINGLETON and EDDIE SNYDER
Music by BERT KAEMPFERT

Moderately slow

Stran - gers in the night _____ ex - chang - ing glanc - es,

won - d'ring in the night _____ what were the chanc - es

we'd be shar - ing love _____ be - fore the night was

through. _____ Some - thing in your eyes _____

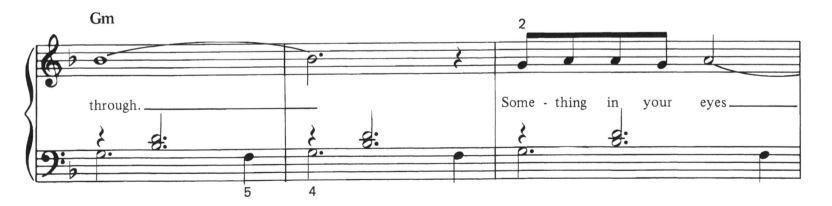

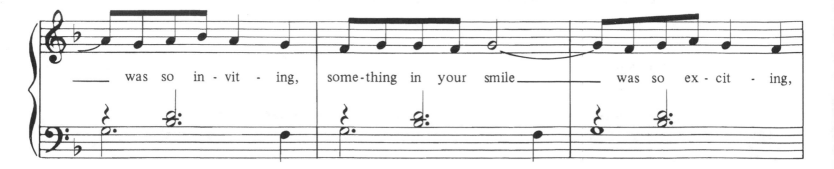

_____ was so in - vit - ing, some-thing in your smile _____ was so ex - cit - ing,

some-thing in my heart _____ told me I must have you. _____

Stran - gers in the night, _____ two lone - ly peo - ple we were.

Stran - gers in the night _____ up to the mo - ment when we

It's Easy to Play Your Favorite Songs with Hal Leonard Easy Piano Books

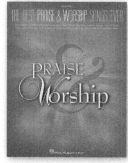

The Best Praise & Worship Songs Ever

The name says it all: over 70 of the best P&W songs today. Titles include: Awesome God • Blessed Be Your Name • Come, Now Is the Time to Worship • Days of Elijah • Here I Am to Worship • Open the Eyes of My Heart • Shout to the Lord • We Fall Down • and more.
00311312 ....$19.99

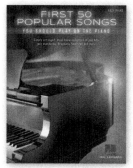

First 50 Popular Songs You Should Play on the Piano

50 great pop classics for beginning pianists to learn, including: Candle in the Wind • Chopsticks • Don't Know Why • Hallelujah • Happy Birthday to You • Heart and Soul • I Walk the Line • Just the Way You Are • Let It Be • Let It Go • Over the Rainbow • Piano Man • and many more.
00131140 ....$16.99

The Greatest Video Game Music

28 easy piano selections for the music that envelops you as you lose yourself in the world of video games, including: Angry Birds Theme • Assassin's Creed Revelations • Dragonborn (Skyrim Theme) • Elder Scrolls: Oblivion • Minecraft: Sweden • Rage of Sparta from God of War III • and more.
00202545 ....$17.99

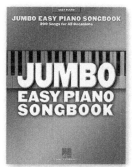

Jumbo Easy Piano Songbook

200 classical favorites, folk songs and jazz standards. Includes: Amazing Grace • Beale Street Blues • Bridal Chorus • Buffalo Gals • Canon in D • Cielito Lindo • Danny Boy • The Entertainer • Für Elise • Greensleeves • Jamaica Farewell • Marianne • Molly Malone • Ode to Joy • Peg O' My Heart • Rockin' Robin • Yankee Doodle • dozens more!
00311014 ....$19.99

Songs from *A Star Is Born*, *The Greatest Showman*, *La La Land*, and More Movie Musicals

Movie musical lovers will delight in this songbook chock full of top-notch songs arranged for easy piano with lyrics from blockbuster movies. Includes: City of Stars from *La La Land* • Suddenly from *Les Misérables* • This Is Me from *The Greatest Showman* • Shallow from *A Star Is Born* • and more.
00287577 ....$17.99

50 Easy Classical Themes

Easy arrangements of 50 classical tunes representing more than 30 composers, including: Bach, Beethoven, Chopin, Debussy, Dvorak, Handel, Haydn, Liszt, Mozart, Mussorgsky, Puccini, Rossini, Schubert, Strauss, Tchaikovsky, Vivaldi, and more.
00311215 ....$14.99

Pop Songs for Kids

Kids from all corners of the world love and sing along to the songs of Taylor Swift, One Direction, Katy Perry, and other pop stars. This collection features 25 songs from these and many more artists in easy piano format. Includes: Brave • Can't Stop the Feeling • Firework • Home • Let It Go • Shake It Off • What Makes You Beautiful • and more.
00221920 ....$14.99

Simple Songs – The Easiest Easy Piano Songs

Play 50 of your favorite songs in the easiest of arrangements! Songs include: Castle on a Cloud • Do-Re-Mi • Happy Birthday to You • Hey Jude • Let It Go • Linus and Lucy • Over the Rainbow • Smile • Star Wars (Main Theme) • Tomorrow • and more.
00142041 ....$14.99

VH1's 100 Greatest Songs of Rock and Roll

The results from the VH1 show that featured the 100 greatest rock and roll songs of all time are here in this awesome collection! Songs include: Born to Run • Good Vibrations • Hey Jude • Hotel California • Imagine • Light My Fire • Like a Rolling Stone • Respect • and more.
00311110 ....$29.99

River Flows in You and Other Eloquent Songs for Easy Piano Solo

24 piano favorites arranged so that even beginning players can sound great. Includes: All of Me • Bella's Lullaby • Cristofori's Dream • Il Postino (The Postman) • Jessica's Theme (Breaking in the Colt) • The John Dunbar Theme • and more.
00137581 ....$14.99

Disney's My First Song Book

16 favorite songs to sing and play. Every page is beautifully illustrated with full-color art from Disney features. Songs include: Beauty and the Beast • Bibbidi-Bobbidi-Boo • Circle of Life • Cruella De Vil • A Dream Is a Wish Your Heart Makes • Hakuna Matata • Under the Sea • Winnie the Pooh • You've Got a Friend in Me • and more.
00310322 ....$17.99

Top Hits of 2019

20 of the year's best are included in this collection arranged for easy piano with lyrics. Includes: Bad Guy (Billie Eilish) • I Don't Care (Ed Sheeran & Justin Bieber) • ME! (Taylor Swift feat. Brendon Urie) • Old Town Road (Remix) (Lil Nas X feat. Billy Ray Cyrus) • Senorita (Shawn Mendes & Camila Cabello) • Someone You Loved (Lewis Capaldi) • and more.
00302273 ....$16.99

Get complete song lists and more at
www.halleonard.com

Prices, contents, and availability subject to change without notice
Disney characters and artwork © Disney Enterprises, Inc.

0320
239